How Do
I Talk
To God?

prayers for
the school year

HOW DO I TALK TO GOD?

prayers for
the school year

Barbara Gargiulo

ThomasMore®
– An RCL Company –

Send all inquiries to:
Thomas More
An RCL Company
200 East Bethany Drive
Allen, Texas 75002-3804

BOOKSTORES:
    Call Bookworld Companies 888-444-2524 or fax 941-753-9396
PARISHES AND SCHOOLS:
    Thomas More Publishing 800-822-6701 or fax 800-688-8356
INTERNATIONAL:
    Fax Thomas More Publishing 972-264-3719

Visit our website at **www.rclweb.com**

Printed in the United States of America

Library of Congress Card Number

ISBN 0-88347-407-7

1 2 3 4 5   03 02 01 00 99

CONTENTS

School Days and Holidays

Autumn Season

Winter Season

Spring Season

Summer Season and Special Occasions

INTRODUCTION

This book offers ideas for prayer at school and uses the special occasions and events of the school year as opportunities for prayer. Of course, these suggestions could be adapted for use at home or at any time or place where young people are gathered.

There are many ways to pray. For some occasions, praying in silence might be the most appropriate way. There might be times when praying aloud a prayer that everyone is familiar with would be more effective. Sometimes we pray from prayer books. Reading Scripture and reflecting on the words is a prayerful experience. At other times, we pray in our own words.

The disciples of Jesus were not known for their quick wit or the speed with which they caught on to things. Yet, one thing they noticed was that Jesus prayed. There were times when Jesus prayed alone. There were other times—before an important event or to call attention to something he was about to do—when Jesus raised his eyes to heaven and put himself in touch with his Father. The disciples became convinced that prayer was important to Jesus. This prompted them to ask, "Lord, teach us to pray."

So, Jesus told his friends some things about prayer. In Matthew 6:5 Jesus tells them, "And when you pray, do not imitate the hypocrites: they love to say their prayers standing up in the synagogues and at the street corners for people to see them. I tell you solemnly they have had their reward. When you pray, go to your room and, when you have shut your door, pray to your Father."

In Matthew 6:7 the disciples listen when Jesus says, "In your prayers do not babble as the pagans do, for they think that by using many words they will make themselves heard. Do not be like them; your Father knows what you need before you ask him. You should pray like this: Our Father in heaven, may your name be held hold your kingdom come, your will be done on earth as in heaven. Give us today our daily bread and forgive us our debts as we have forgiven those who are in debt to us. And do not put us to the test but save us from the evil one."

In Matthew 7:7 Jesus says, "Ask and it will be given to you, search, and you will find; knock and the door will be opened to you." In Matthew 18:7 Jesus teaches, ". . . if two of you on earth agree to ask anything at all, it will be granted to you by my Father in heaven. For where two or three meet in my name, I shall be there with them."

Students should be encouraged to bring their petitions and their requests for prayer. Assure them that God is interested in them and in the details of their lives. No concern is too trivial or unimportant. Each individual might find a special place for prayer and a best time for prayer. Music should certainly be a part of prayer. The class might try different postures and gestures during prayer. In the classroom, prayer does not always have to come at the beginning of the day. In the middle of a lesson, a teacher or a catechist might suggest, "Let's stop now and pray about that."

Jesus taught his disciples about prayer. He also teaches us about prayer. Recognizing the importance of prayer, we help our students pray. We can do this in many ways—by modeling prayer, by praying with them, and by talking with them about prayer.

AUTUMN SEASON

From the First Day of School
to the First Sunday of Advent

The book of Ecclesiastes assures us that "There is an appointed time for everything and a time for every affair under the heavens." (3:1)

This autumn time, this beginning of the school year, is a time for learning about one another. Learning names is important. Learning habits and moods and routines are also at the top of the list. We all need to be convinced that God knows us and loves us individually and personally.

Autumn is also the season for establishing a prayer place and assembling props and materials that will aid in prayer. (On a very practical note, educators take differing views about the presence of candles in the room. Some say NEVER; others simply encourage the adult in charge to be watchful and to extinguish the candle as soon as prayer is over.)

Allow students to experiment with pray postures (sitting, standing, kneeling) and gestures (arms raised or outstretched, eyes closed). Ask students to be prayer readers and also to suggest and select prayers.

This season includes special holidays, Halloween and All Saints Day. The children will be very excited about these events and will usually find ways to celebrate with prayer.

As the earth becomes quiet and dormant, we can look to prayer to be a quieting, centering experience. As the autumn gives splashes of beautiful color, our prayer can reflect the colors of our lives and personalities. Students will enjoy learning about one another and assuming various places within the class community.

FIRST DAY OF SCHOOL

Jeremiah 18:1–4

" . . . I went down to the
potter's house and there he was,
working at the wheel. Whenever the
object of clay which he was making
turned out badly in his hand, he
tried again, making of the clay
another object of whatever
sort he pleased."

A new school year is like formless clay in our hands. We can make of it whatever we please. The possibilities are infinite. If we make a mistake, we can start over. We can try again.

JESUS,

We are excited to be here on the first day of school! We are glad to meet new friends and to learn new things. As we go through this year, please help us to be kind to one another and to welcome the new people who will come to this school. Bless our teacher and our families. Open our minds and our hearts so that we can understand new things about ourselves, about you, and about your wonderful creation.

Amen.

LABOR DAY WEEKEND

Luke 10:2

"[Jesus] said to them, 'The harvest
is abundant but the laborers are
few; so ask the master of the
harvest to send out laborers for
the harvest.' "

This is a good time to reflect on the dignity
and value of hard work. Jesus tells us that
there is much work to be done. We need to be
aware of the importance of our contribution
and effort toward the bringing about of God's
kingdom.

GOD, OUR FATHER,

There is no school on Monday. We have a long weekend. Some of us will be going on picnics. Some of us will be taking long trips away from home to visit family and friends who live far away. Please keep us safe and bring us back here next Tuesday morning. Bless all people who work hard. This is a weekend to honor them.

Amen.

[You may ask different children to read the following.]
We thank you Lord for these first days of school. Let us pray to the Lord.
[All: Lord, hear our prayer.]
For our parents who work hard. Let us pray to the Lord.
[All: Lord, hear our prayer.]
For all who are traveling this weekend. Let us pray to the Lord.
[All: Lord, hear our prayer.]

Invite children to offer their own petitions.

AUTUMN

Luke 12:54–55

"[Jesus] also said to the crowds,
'When you see [a] cloud rising in
the west you say . . . it is going to
rain—and so it does; and when
you notice that the wind is blowing
from the south you say that it is
going to be hot—and so it is.'"

In these verses, Jesus tells us it is important to look for and understand the signs around us. Just as we know that natural signs—leaves changing color, days becoming shorter, winds becoming colder—reveal the coming of autumn, there are also signs of God in our lives. We need to recognize and respond to them.

LORD GOD,

We know that you made all things—the trees, the birds, the beautiful sky. You must be very beautiful because the trees and the birds flying in large flocks are so beautiful. Thank you for this wonderful season of autumn and for all the things we can learn about you.

Amen.

HALLOWEEN

Mark 6:47–50

"When it was evening the boat was far out
on the sea and [Jesus] was alone on shore.
Then he saw that they were tossed about
while rowing, for the wind was against them.
About the fourth watch of the night, he
came toward them walking on the sea. . . .
When they saw him walking on the sea, they
thought it was a ghost, and cried out. They
had all seen him and were terrified. But at
once he spoke with them, 'Take courage,
it is I, do not be afraid!' "

We don't need to be afraid of anything.
Jesus is our strength, our courage, stronger
than any fear we might have.

LORD JESUS,

Today is Halloween. We have special costumes to wear and parties to attend. There are pumpkins and ghosts everywhere! Please be with us as we have fun and enjoy each other. Thank you for our parents because they have done many things to help us enjoy this day. Stay with us; it will be so much fun!

Amen.

ALL SAINTS DAY

Matthew 25:34–40

"...Then the king will say to those on his right, 'Come you who are blessed by my Father. Inherit the kingdom prepared for you from the foundation of the world. For I was hungry and you gave me food, I was thirsty and you gave me drink, ...'"

Saints are people who care for other people. There are those who are canonized by the Church; there are those who live and work among us.

DEAR GOD,

Today is the feast of your holy saints. Saints are people who obey you and do your will. They show us how to live. Please help us to know more about your saints, especially the saints for whom we are named. Through their lives, these saints show us how to live and how to be pleasing to you. We know that some of our own family members are saints. We want to learn from them. Thank you for giving us holy people.

Amen.

WINTER SEASON

From the First Sunday of Advent
to the First Day of Spring

Winter is the season of traditions and special celebrations. Students will be very excited about the coming of Christmas. Plans for visitors, travel, and gifts are all part of the daily scene. It would be good to use this excitement in prayer.

This is also the season of gifts. Saint Paul assures us that we all have spiritual gifts. In 1 Corinthians 12 we learn that there are many kinds of spiritual gifts. These are bestowed through the Spirit so that the individual and the community might benefit.

Prayer can help us discern our gifts and can help us be generous in using these gifts for the benefit of others. Offering prayers of thanksgiving for our own gifts and for the gifts of others is an important way to celebrate.

During this time we think of Mary, the mother of Jesus, in a special way. Offering opportunities for special celebrations, like Eucharistic celebrations, is appropriate. The feast of Mary's Immaculate Conception is December 8. January 1 is the solemnity of Mary. Our Lady of Guadalupe and her appearance to Juan Diego is celebrated on December 9. This feast is especially important to Hispanic Christians.

Involve the students in planning and decision-making about prayer. This is also a good time with the beginning of Lent to use Jesus as a model of prayer. Jesus prayed at his baptism (Luke 3:21). Jesus prayed in the desert (Luke 4:1) and he prayed over the loaves and fishes (Luke 9:16). Jesus prayed before calling his friend Lazarus out of the tomb (John 11:39). Jesus prayed the night before he died (John 22:39) and Jesus prayed on the cross (Luke 23:34 and Luke 23:46). Jesus prayed and gave us an example of how to pray.

A special holiday during this season, Saint Valentine's Day (February 14), can lead us into prayers of love. This is a good time to introduce the idea that our actions might also be prayers. Actions that tell of our love for God and for other people can be our best prayers.

WINTER

Ecclesiastes 3:1

"There is an appointed time for everything, and a time for every affair under the heaven."

Winter is the time when nature recoups strength and life. Farming soils can rest, animals can hibernate, and plants can be rejuvenated. Rest and quiet beauty are the order of the days.

DEAR GOD,

When we woke up this morning there was snow outside. We wanted to stay out all day and play and build snowmen, but we will have to wait until after school. Snow is so much fun. Thank you for sleds, ice skates, and snow. Thank you for boots and for warm clothes to wear. Thank you for letting us have fun together.

Amen.

THANKSGIVING

Luke 17:11–19

" . . . As [the ten lepers] were going
they were cleansed. And one of
them, realizing he had been healed,
returned, glorifying God in a loud
voice; and he fell at the feet of
Jesus and thanked him . . ."

Jesus praised the man who said "thank
you." Jesus asked, "Ten were cleansed, were
they not? Where are the other nine?"

Let us remember the importance of
thanking God and all those who support and
help us.

Read the story of the ten lepers in Luke 17, then pray:

LORD JESUS,

You were pleased with the one man who came back to say, "Thank you." Saying "thank you" is important. Please help us to remember to say "thank you" to all the people who do good things for us—especially our parents. And thank you for all the gifts you give us each day.

Amen.

ADVENT

Luke 13:18–21

"... the kingdom of God is like a
mustard seed that a person took
and planted in the garden. ...
It is like yeast that a woman took
and mixed [in] with ... wheat flour
until the whole batch of dough
was leavened."

In these verses, Jesus speaks of the mustard seed growing into a large tree so large birds can build nests in the branches of the tree. Then Jesus tells of the woman who bakes bread; she buries yeast in the measures of flour. In both examples, Jesus is speaking of something that takes time. Both things are hard to wait for, yet neither can be hurried. Some things are very hard to wait for; some things are worth waiting for. We want Christmas to come; we pray that we can wait patiently.

DEAR GOD,

Dark blue is the color of Advent. It is in Church and we have three dark blue candles and one pink candle at school. This is a special time of getting ready for Christmas. We want to make sure that our hearts are ready for your birth on Christmas. Please let us listen well to the Bible stories and to all the things you did to help us prepare for your Son Jesus. As the light of our candles gets brighter and brighter, help us to be ready for Christmas.

Amen.

CHRISTMAS

1 John 4:10

"In this is love: not that we
have loved God, but that he
loved us and sent his Son as
expiation for our sins."

This is our meditation for Christmas: God loved the world so much, he loved us so much, that he sent his son as a perfect and fitting way of accomplishing our salvation. We did nothing to deserve this; it is a gift from God to us.

DEAR GOD,

At last, Christmas is here! Today is the last day of class. We have Christmas vacation. The food is very good. Grandma and Grandpa are coming. I will spend some quiet time just looking at our manger scene at home. I like to think about how you were a little baby in Bethlehem and how the animals kept you warm. Thank you for Christmas trees and for Christmas presents. This is a wonderful time!

Amen.

THE NEW YEAR

Genesis 1:1–2

"In the beginning, when God
created the heavens and the earth,
the earth was a formless
wasteland, and darkness covered
the abyss . . ."

This new year is formless and dark. It is waiting for our energy and our action. We pray that we are not just reactors but rather are hard-working agents dedicated to the coming of God's kingdom.

JESUS,

You make all things new. We are happy to have this new year. We hope this new year will bring many good days for our friends and for our families. We know that you will be with us and will help all of us through this year. We want to be your holy people.

Amen.

GROUND HOG DAY

Luke 21:29–30

"He taught them a lesson.
'Consider the fig tree and all the
other trees. When their buds burst
open, you see for yourselves and
know that summer is now near . . .' "

We wait anxiously for signs of spring—the
return of certain birds, the appearance of
buds and emerging plants. We pray that we
are attentive to God's earth and the role we
have as stewards of God's creation.

DEAR GOD,

Some people call them woodchucks, and some people call them groundhogs. They are cute furry animals. There is a special groundhog in Pennsylvania. People watch him on February 2. Some people think that this groundhog tells how long winter will be. Some years the groundhog is right, but other years the groundhog is wrong. Thank you anyway for them. They are cute and fun to watch.

Amen.

VALENTINE'S DAY

1 Corinthians 13:4–8

"Love is patient, love is kind. It is
not jealous, [love]is not pompous,
it is not inflated, it is not rude, it
does not seek its own interests,
it is not quick-tempered, it does
not brood over injury, it does not
rejoice over wrongdoing but
rejoices with the truth. It bears
all things, believes all things, hopes
all things, endures all things.
Love never fails . . ."

Let us pray that our flowers, candy, paper
hearts are expressions of the real love we hold
for other people.

Read a story of Saint Valentine from a book of saints, then pray,

DEAR GOD,

Today is Valentine's Day. Saint Valentine is your special saint, and we read a story about him. I made notes and cards to send to all the people I love. Today is a day when we take some time to send messages of love to people. Help us to remember to say, "I love you" every day.

Amen.

A WINDY DAY

Acts 2:1–2

"When the time for Pentecost was
fulfilled, they were all in one place
together. And suddenly there came
from the sky a noise like a strong
driving wind, and it filled the entire
house in which they were."

The Spirit took the form of a wind, filled the
house and filled the lives of the apostles of
Jesus. They were transformed; they were no
longer afraid. Let us pray that we are open to
the spirit and that windy days can remind us
of how the spirit comes into our lives and
transforms us.

DEAR GOD,

Today is so windy I really had to hold onto my hat while I was walking to school. Today we are going to make kites. We will tie them to a ball of string and see if they will fly. Thank you for letting us learn about wind in science class. We are glad you made air for us to breathe and wind to bring in fresh air. Thank you for thinking of wind.

Amen.

SPRING SEASON

From the First Day of Spring
to the Last Day of School

The Easter and Pentecost season is a time for celebrating the salvation that Jesus accomplished for us through his death. By this time, students will know and feel comfortable with one another. It might be the occasion for the celebration of a sacrament such as First Eucharist or Reconciliation of Confirmation. This is the season when important liturgical rites and ceremonies become part of prayer.

The end of the school year is always very busy. There are special tests to take and ceremonies and traditions to be observed. People are tired and hassled and need the strength that prayer can offer. This might be a good time to read the story of the persistent widow (Luke 18:1–8). This story encourages us to be steadfast in our prayer, to not give up.

The natural events of spring would be useful in telling the Easter story—Bringing in branches that appear dead and watching them sprout (Forsythia is good if it is available.) and planting bulbs and watching the hyacinths or tulips emerge are great examples that would teach the children that Jesus is alive.

The Spring season is a time for thinking about those qualities that make a person a good pray-er. A good pray-er is one who makes the time to pray. "Here I am, Lord. Your servant is listening." A good pray-er is honest with God. Remember that both Moses and the prophet Jeremiah objected. They told God, "I am not a good speaker" (to say nothing of the fact that Moses was wanted for murder and if he went back to Egypt he would probably be arrested) and "I am too young." In both of these instances, God praised the pray-er for being honest but also said that excuses were not allowed. This brings up another quality of a good pray-er, that of open listening and willingness to change. God says, "I am not asking you to do something that is too hard for you. Know that I will be with you." It is good to ask how we can help ourselves and our students develop these qualities of availability, openness, and trust in God.

SPRING BREAK

Matthew 11:28–30

"Come to me, all you who labor and
are burdened, and I will give you
rest. Take my yoke upon you and
learn from me, for I am meek and
humble of heart; and you will find
rest for yourselves. For my yoke is
easy, and my burden light."

When we crave the rest of a vacation, let us
remember the words of Jesus that if we come
to him, he will calm us and give us rest.

DEAR GOD,

Springtime is so beautiful. The flowers and trees are blooming. The spring and summer birds are coming back. The weather is warm and it feels good to be outside. Thank you for some vacation days so that we can enjoy this beautiful time. Thank you for giving us this time to be with one another. It's very hard to choose, but I think of all your seasons, I like spring the best.

Amen.

A RAINY DAY

John 7:37–38

"On the last and greatest day of
the feast, Jesus stood up and
exclaimed, 'Let anyone who thirsts
come to me and drink. Whoever
believes in me, as scripture says,
Rivers of living water will flow
from within him.' "

As we watch rain fall and we see the thirsty
ground soak up the nourishing moisture, let
us remember that Jesus has promised us
that rivers of living water will flow from our
belief in him.

DEAR GOD,

Raincoats and umbrellas are dripping everywhere. Your earth and all living things need water. Today the rain is really coming down. Rainy days give us time to be quiet and to think about you and your wonderful gifts. Rain is very calm and peaceful. Thank you for rain—but please don't let it last too long.

Amen.

EASTER

Luke 24:1–6

"But at daybreak on the first day of the week they took the spices they had prepared and went to the tomb. They found the stone rolled away from the tomb; but when they entered, they did not find the body of the Lord Jesus. While they were puzzling over this, behold, two men in dazzling garments appeared to them. They were terrified and bowed their faces to the ground. They said to them, 'Why do you seek the living one among the dead? He is not here, but he has been raised.' "

Alleluia.

Read Luke 24:1 or another "empty tomb" gospel. Then pray,

JESUS,

Your friends looked for you in the tomb where you had been buried. You weren't there. At first, they wondered if your body had been stolen, but then you appeared and explained to them that you are more powerful than death. You are alive! Your friends were happy. We are happy. Easter is a very special day.

Amen.

FLOWERS

Luke 12:27

"Notice how the flowers grow. They
do not toil or spin. But I tell you,
not even Solomon in all his splendor
was dressed like one of them."

Jesus tells us that God cares for flowers and has made them very beautiful. As we appreciate the beauty of the spring flowers, let us also appreciate the beauty of God and his care for us.

DEAR GOD,

Today we brought some flowers to school. We looked at them quietly and thought about how beautiful they are. They are bright and colorful. The flowers smell good. You must be very beautiful because you made these beautiful flowers.

Amen.

MONTH OF MAY

Luke 1:38

"Mary said, 'Behold, I am the
handmaid of the Lord.
May it be done to me according
to your word.' "

Mary did not exactly understand what God was asking; in human terms it made no sense. Yet her faith was so strong she said, Whatever God wills is all right with me. We pray that with Mary as our example and model, we can strengthen our own faith and say "yes" to God.

DEAR GOD,

May is a special month here at school. We have many special events and occasions. We have concerts and programs and end-of-the-year assemblies. Everyone is very busy. Please help us never to be too busy to pray to you. We know you are here with us.

Amen.

MOTHERS' DAY

John 19:26–27

"When Jesus saw his mother and
the disciple there whom he loved,
he said to his mother, 'Woman,
behold, your son.' Then he said to
the disciple, 'Behold, your mother.'
And from that hour the disciple
took her into his home."

As we celebrate Mothers' Day, we pray
that we honor those who are mothers. We
remember that Jesus gave us his mother as
our protector and example.

JESUS,

Your mother's name is Mary. Today we have written the name of each of our mothers on a piece of paper, and we have put those names in a special place in the room. Bless all mothers. Please help me to let my mother know how much I love and appreciate her. She does so many good things for me. I want to do good things for her, too.

Amen.

MEMORIAL DAY

Matthew 8: 8–10

"The centurion said in reply, 'Lord, I am not worthy to have you enter under my roof; only say the word and my servant will be healed. For I too am a person subject to authority, with soldiers subject to me. And I say to one, 'Go,' and he goes; and to another, 'Come here.' and he comes; and to my slave, 'Do this,' and he does it. When Jesus heard this, he was amazed and said to those following him, 'Amen, I say to you, in no one in Israel have I found such faith.' "

As we remember those who have fought for our country we listen to the centurion describe being a soldier. We pray that God will bless and protect those in the military and will bring to himself those who have died serving their country.

DEAR GOD,

Summer is almost here. This is memorial day weekend. We are honoring the brave people who defended our country when our country was at war. Thank you for the lives of these people. We thank you today for the lives of all brave and courageous people. We know there are many different ways to be strong and brave. We want to learn to be people of courage.

Amen.

TAKING A TEST

Matthew 7:7–8

"Ask and it will be given to you;
seek and you will find; knock and
the door will be opened to you. For
everyone who asks, receives; and
the one who seeks, finds; and to
the one who knocks, the door
will be opened."

Let us remember that after we have studied, after we have put forth our best effort, Jesus has assured us of the power of prayer. We pray for big things and for little things. We ask God to be present in whatever we do.

62

DEAR GOD,

Today we have to take achievement tests. Our teacher says that these tests will help us to know what we learned this year. Please help us to do our best and to not be nervous during these tests. Help us to read each question carefully and then to mark the best answer. Sometimes tests can help us learn.

Amen.

THE LAST DAY OF SCHOOL

John 19:30

"When Jesus had taken the wine,
he said, 'It is finished.' And
bowing his head, he handed
over the spirit."

We pray that as we come to the end of a
school year, we can say, "I have done my best.
I have accomplished what I set out to do. This
is work I am proud of. I offer it to God."

DEAR JESUS,

This school year is over. We have learned many new things about each other and about our school subjects. Thank you for letting us be the people we are. Thank you for our teachers and all the hard work they have done. Please help us have a safe and fun summer. We will be glad to see each other again next fall.

Amen.

SUMMER SEASON
AND SPECIAL OCCASIONS

Ordinary Time

Hopefully, our job is well done and our students will have the experience and the skills to pray themselves through the summer. This is the season for having the time and the energy to pray and to really appreciate our relationship with God. This is the time to see God in nature—an ocean, a mountain, a forest. This is the season to be with family and friends, to appreciate individual persons and to learn more about them.

Like other seasons, the summertime has prayers for special occasions, like Fathers' Day; times of birth and times of death; prayers for experiences such as meeting a new neighbor who will be part of the class when the school year begins; and prayers for visitors and for vacationers. Even though this season is called Ordinary Time in the liturgical year, the events and happenings of the season may not be ordinary at all.

Summer is the time for learning new things about ourselves and for relaxing with the time to enjoy this whole process. It's the season for writing down our prayer experiences in a diary or journal. Journal entries can consist of letters to God or letters to ourselves. They can begin this way: Today I hope that . . . ; What I really want to tell my friend . . . ; or What I want God to know is . . . .

Encourage the children to write down their thoughts on a daily basis by giving them a small notebook as an end-of-the-year gift. With the refreshment of summer and with the clarification offered by a prayer journal, you and the children will be ready to begin the next school year.

FATHERS' DAY

Ephesians 6:1–4

"Children, obey your parents [in the
Lord], for this is right. Honor your
father and mother. . . . Fathers, do
not provoke your children to anger,
but bring them up with the training
and instruction of the Lord."

JESUS,

Thank you for showing us that God is our father as well as your father. Today we also especially thank you for our earthly fathers. I am grateful for the time my father spends with me. He gives me many special gifts. I ask you to give my dad your blessing today and every day.

Amen.

FAMILY VACATION

Job 38, 39

"Then the Lord addressed Job out of
the storm and said: . . . 'Where were
you when I founded the earth? Tell
me, if you have understanding. . . .' "

In these two chapters of the Old
Testament, God questions Job about his
knowledge of nature and creation. God asks
Job about mountains and about the sea. He
asks Job about plants and animals and the
details of their lives. Job cannot answer.

Vacations are times for us to appreciate
God's creation. We can look at the mountains,
the forests, the oceans and learn about God
and his ways.

JESUS,

Today we leave for our vacation. Please be with us as we travel. Bring us home safely when our vacation is over. We pray that we will enjoy this time of rest and will learn more about you and your Father. Help us to see you in your beautiful creation and in the people you love.

Amen.

BIRTHDAY

Jeremiah 1:5

"Before I formed you in the womb
I knew you, before you were born
I dedicated you. . . ."

God assures us that he knows each one of
us very well and that he has an individual plan
for each one of us. He has known us and has
been interested in our lives since before we
were born. A birthday is a day to celebrate the
uniqueness of each person and to reflect on
God's special care for each one of us.

DEAR GOD OUR FATHER,

Today is _____'s birthday. We know that each one of us is special to you. You call us by our name and consider each of us to be your friend. Today bless _____, and help him (her) to have a truly happy day. Let us show our love and our care and how much we thank you for this birthday person.

Amen.

WHEN SOMEONE IS SICK

Mark 1:32–34

"When it was evening, after sunset,
they brought to him all who were ill
or possessed by demons. The whole
town was gathered at the door. He
cured many who were sick with
various diseases, and he drove out
many demons . . ."

Let us remember the power of Jesus to cure and heal. Jesus helped those who were brought to him and those who asked for his help. Let us pray that those who are sick are touched by his healing power and know his kindness and his presence.

DEAR JESUS,

We have read many gospel stories about how you cure sick people. We know that _____ is sick. Please touch him (her) with your healing power. Please help all who are ill to feel and know your presence. Be with them and restore their health soon.

Amen.

WHEN SOMEONE DIES

John 11:25–26

"Jesus told her, 'I am the
resurrection and the life; whoever
believes in me, even if he dies, will
live, and everyone who lives and
believes in me will never die.
Do you believe this?'"

We do not understand death; we find it
overwhelming. We are left with the question of
Jesus—Do you believe that those who believe
in me will never die?

JESUS,

You said that those who believe in you will live on even after they die. We don't know exactly what that means, but we are thinking about it today because we just heard that _____ has died. We ask you to lead this person right to heaven and to comfort his (her) family and friends. They are feeling so sad. Help them and help all of us to remember your words.

Amen.

A BIRTH IN THE FAMILY

Luke 1:57–58

"When the time arrived for
Elizabeth to have her child she gave
birth to a son. Her neighbors and
relatives heard that the Lord had
shown his great mercy toward her,
and they rejoiced with her."

The birth of a baby brings great excitement. Who is this person? What will he or she become? We pray for this unique and special person and for all those who will influence this new life.

DEAR JESUS,

We are so excited because _____ has a new baby boy (girl). We thank you for this gift of life. We know that each person is your special friend and that you love each one of us. We wonder who this baby will grow up to be. We will pray for this person, and we will be a friend as he (she) gets bigger.

Amen.

GRANDPARENTS

Sirach 3:12–14

"My son, take care of your father when
he is old; grieve him not as long as
he lives. Even if his mind fail, be
considerate with him; revile him not
in the fullness of your strength.
For kindness to a father will not be
forgotten, it will serve as a sin
offering—it will take lasting root."

Earth's population is aging. People are living longer. Many of today's grandparents are healthy and active and involved in the lives of their grandchildren. For this we are very grateful. We respect the wisdom and grace that come with age. We teach children that even if grandparents become old or sick or do "funny things" they deserve our love and our care.

DEAR GOD,

My grandmother and grandfather are so good to me. They spend time listening to me, taking me places and coming to my activities at school. They come to my soccer game and clap when I score a goal. They read really great books to me and watch me when my mom and dad are away. I am so glad that I know them. Please watch over my grandmother and grandfather with your special care. Keep them healthy and give them long lives.

Amen.

VISITORS

Luke 10:38–42

"As they continued their journey he entered a village where a woman whose name was Martha welcomed him. She had a sister named Mary [who] sat beside the Lord at his feet listening to him speak. Martha, burdened with much serving, came to him and said, 'Lord, do you not care that my sister has left me by myself to do the serving? Tell her to help me.' The Lord said to her in reply, 'Martha, Martha, you are anxious and worried about many things. There is need of only one thing. Mary has chosen the better part and it will not be taken from her.'"

Visits from grandparents, relatives, friends are exciting. Let us remember that hospitality is an expression of Christian life. Kindness toward and care for those who visit us is a way of loving our neighbor. Listening to and trying to understand those who visit can improve our own lives.

DEAR GOD,

We like to have company. It is always exciting when someone comes to visit. Sometimes it's Grandma and Grandpa, sometimes it's other families or friends. We want to be kind to people who visit us. Help us to work very hard to help them feel at home. These are your special people and you want us to love them.

Amen.

A NEW JOB

Matthew 20:3–4

*"Going out about nine o'clock, he
saw others standing idle in the
marketplace, and he said to them,
'You too go into my vineyard, and
I will give you what is just.'"*

We are happy for those who find meaningful work, new opportunities and gainful employment. We can imagine the workers in Matthew's gospel needing and hoping to find work. How happy we are for those who seek and find a new job.

DEAR GOD,

_____ has a new job. We know this is both exciting and scary. New things are like that. We ask your special help for this person as he (she) learns new things and meets new people. We are grateful for work and the chance to use our talents. Give your special blessings to those who are starting something new.

Amen.

MEETING SOMEONE NEW IN CLASS

Matthew 25:35

"For I was . . . a stranger and you welcomed me . . ."

It is so hard for young people to move to a new place and to find new friends. Jesus says that the kindness we show to strangers will be rewarded.

DEAR GOD,

You have said that when we welcome other people, we welcome you. Today we have a new person in our class. His (Her) name is _____ .
We know that you love him (her) and that he (she) is your special friend. Help us to be kind and to learn all the great things about this new friend. We want new people to feel welcome and to quickly become a part of our class.

Amen.

SOMEONE MOVING AWAY

Genesis 12:1

"The Lord said to Abram, 'Go forth
from the land of your kinsfolk and
from your father's house to a land
that I will show you.' "

When the circumstances of our lives bring us to a new place, we pray that we will find God's call and His will for us. The excitement of a new place and a new beginning can be part of God's plan. Let us pray that we listen to God's voice.

DEAR GOD,

_____ is moving to

_____ . We are sad,
and we are really going to miss him
(her). We had so much fun together,
and we helped each other. Please
help us to stay in touch and to know
that we have a friend in a new place.

Amen.

A PRIZE OR AWARD

John 19:11

"Jesus answered [him] [Pilate],
'You would have no power over me
if it had not been given to you
from above.' "

Let us be aware of the fact that honors and awards bestowed on us come not only from our own effort and hard work but also from God. Let us pray that we use our talents and our gifts for God and for others. Let us be humble in acknowledging God's part in our achievements.

92

DEAR JESUS,

We have just learned that _____ has won a special award. We know that you help us and are with us in all that we do. We are grateful for this recognition and for all the people who helped us achieve it. We thank you and we thank

_____ .

Amen.

SCHOOL ATHLETIC TEAMS

2 Timothy 4:7–8

"I have competed well; I have
finished the race; I have kept the
faith. From now on the crown of
righteousness awaits me . . ."

An athlete can be justly proud of the
accomplishments gained through persistent
training and difficult competition. Paul
reminds us that life is like an athletic contest.
We work hard. We run the race. We earn the
reward.

DEAR GOD,

Our team has a big game today. Please help us to do our best and to play fair. We want to play by the rules and win fair and square. We know our opponents are good and will be trying hard. Keep us from injury and most of all, help us to have fun as we play this game.

Amen.